ELDER WILLIAM BREWSTER,

OF THE "MAYFLOWER:"

HIS BOOKS AND AUTOGRAPHS,

With Other Notes.

By JUSTIN WINSOR.

REPRINTED, SEVENTY-FIVE COPIES, FROM THE PROCEEDINGS, MARCH, 1887,
OF THE MASSACHUSETTS HISTORICAL SOCIETY.

CAMBRIDGE:
JOHN WILSON AND SON.
University Press.
1887.

BOOKS AND AUTOGRAPHS

OF

ELDER WILLIAM BREWSTER,

WITH OTHER NOTES.

Mr. Winsor said : —

When recently investigating the details of the famous Indian fight of Captain Lovewell near Fryeburg, Maine, May 8, 1725, I was obliged to accept the map of the neighborhood of the pond on the banks of which the conflict took place, as it is given in Bouton's edition of "Lovewell's Great Fight," (Concord, New Hampshire, 1861), and copied in Frederick Kidder's "Expedition of Captain John Lovewell" (Boston, 1865). This map places the scene at the north angle of the pond, as deduced from the accounts and traditions. Since I made this study I have found an early plan entered upon the records of Harvard College[1] by President Langdon, with care enough to indicate an accurate copy "from a large plan belonging to the proprietors of Fryeburg." This draught shows "Lovels pond",and its neighborhood, and there is a small dot put against the shore on the northeast side of the pond with this inscription, " Place of Lovel's battle with the Indians." This plan must have been made not many years from 1770, or about forty years after the event, when there were many persons living remembering the occurrence.

Langdon, it will be remembered, was a map-maker not without experience, for he had assisted Colonel Blanchard in the well-known map of New Hampshire which was published in 1761.

[1] College Book, vol. iii. p. 130.

Mr. WINSOR also said : —

I have had occasion in another place to review the discussions which have taken place over the landfall of Sir Francis Drake on the California coast, in connection with the views of our associate, Dr. Hale, that San Francisco Bay was the spot.[1] I received yesterday from Professor George Davidson, of the Coast Survey, an abstract of a paper read by him before the California Academy of Sciences, on the "Early Spanish Voyages of Discovery on the Coast of California." As his conclusions on the point of Drake's landing are at variance with what has usually been held by his associates in the Survey, and as he has been on work in the coast line of that region for more than thirty-five years, his opinion is of importance to any one who seeks to weigh the evidence. His testimony is in favor of what is known as Jack's Bay, or the Sir Francis Drake Bay of the modern maps, which is a depression in the coast a few miles north of the Golden Gate. He identifies the " Portus Novæ Albionis " of Drake, given by that navigator as under 38° of north latitude, with the " Baia de Pinos " of Cabrillo, the " Bahia de los Pinos " of Ferrelo, the " Puerto de San Francisco " of Vizcaino, and holds them to be the modern Drake's Bay, or the northern part of the gulf of the Farallones, whose true latitude is precisely what Drake records, and more than a degree south of the record made by Ferrelo.

Those interested in the historical cartography of the Pacific coast will be glad to learn that Professor Davidson in this paper has sought to determine the identity of sixty-nine places on the coast mentioned in the narratives of Ulloa, Cabrillo, Ferrelo, Drake, and Vizcaino, and that, as the result of much study, it has been submitted to the Superintendent of the United States Coast and Geodetic Survey for publication.

Mr. WINSOR finally referred to the list of the nearly four hundred books left by Elder William Brewster of the " Mayflower " at his death, as interesting in showing what the most ·learned man of that company had gathered for his household companions. He said : —

This list is spread upon the records of inventories at Plymouth,[2] and enables us to authenticate all of the auto-

1 Narrative and Critical History of America, vol. lii. p. 74.
2 Plymouth Wills, vol. i. p. 53.

graphs of the Elder which are known, with the exception of one, and that is attached to the record of a deed in the Court House at Plymouth, — not a solitary instance in those records of original signatures being attached to papers spread upon its records, — and this was for a long time the only autograph of Brewster known. About thirty years ago a copy of Cartwright's "Harmonia Evangelica" (Amsterdam, 1627), was found in the Yale College Library, — the same book priced in the inventory at Plymouth at five shillings. It has, accompanying the signature, the motto "Hebel est omnis Adam," which seems to be play upon the Hebrew names of Adam and Abel and to signify the vanity or transitoriness of man. Not long after this a folio Chrysostom (Basle, 1522) was discovered in the Boston Athenæum, with the name and motto, and it was found to be further inscribed as having been owned by the young Thomas Prince, a son of Governor Prince, who married a daughter of Brewster, and also as having been at one time the property of President Wadsworth of Harvard College. Brewster died in April, 1644, and young Prince notes receiving it in July following thus: "Thomæ Principis. Liber ex bibliotheca avi mei, 1644, Jull." Some years later than this a copy of Francis Johnson's "Treatise of the Ministery of the Church of England" (1595) came into the hands of a Boston dealer, and thence passed to our associate, Dr. Dexter, who has given a fac-simile of the autograph of Brewster which it contains, in his "Literature of Congregationalism" (p. 410). It is not accompanied by the motto, and has a firmer stroke in the writing, so that it is probably an earlier date than the others. This as well as the Athenæum volume is also in the inventory.

At the time I made a note on these autographs in the "History of America" (vol. iii. p. 287) no others were thought to be known; but two additional have since come to my knowledge. The first of these is in one of the Commentaries of David Pareus, of which the inventory shows three, including this, which is the "In Genesin Mosis Commentarius" (Frankfort, 1615). This also has the motto, and belongs to Mr. William Brewster, the ornithologist, my neighbor at Cambridge. The other of these last two is found in a volume which I chanced upon a few months ago in Woodstock, Connecticut, and it proves to be of accumulated interest for the series of autographs which it contains. The inventory at Plymouth shows "Senecas Workes, 6 shillings," and the book in question is this folio volume, being Thomas Lodge's English translation of Seneca's Morals, published in London in 1614. It seems to have been owned at first by two persons named Kyrbie, of whom I can find nothing, the autographs being "Edmund Kyrbie, anno domini, 1614," "Edward Kyrbye," and in a latinized form "Edvardus Kyrbie." Its interest begins with the next signature, "William Peirse his book," — the master mariner who commanded the "Ann," which brought Edward Winslow to Plymouth in 1623, and who after that date is frequently found on the coast, now serving the Pilgrims and then the Massachusetts people. It will be remembered that Winthrop found him and his ship in Gloucester Harbor when he first touched the New England coast in 1630, and fired "two ordnance" in salutation. It will be remembered, too, that the almanac of "Mr. William Peirse mariner" was the first thing printed at Cambridge in 1639, after the little broadside of the "Freeman's Oath." How Peirse's book wandered after it arrived we learn from the next inscription: "Willm. Brewster, his booke, bought of William Peirse. Cost 10/6, in Plimouth in New England. Hebel est omnis Adam." Brewster, as I have said, died in 1644, when the book fell to his son Love Brewster, and was by him sold the same year to the eldest son of Myles Standish, as is shown by the autograph "Alexander Standish, his booke, bought of Love Brewster, cost 16ˢ — 1644." The next signature is of David Standish, a son of Alexander; but it was from another son of Alexander that it passed to the hands of the minister of Duxbury, — "John Robinson, his Book, 1722, bought of Thomas Standish." The next transmission was on a death-bed, for Robinson died on the same day noted in the next autograph, — "Ichabod Robinson's Book. The gift of his Rev. Father Mr. John Robinson Nov. 14, 1745." John Robinson at the time of his death was living in Lebanon, Connecticut, which was the home of Jonathan Trumbull, the later Governor of Connecticut, who had married a daughter of Robinson. Trumbull's daughter married William Williams, the Connecticut signer of the Declaration of Independence; and through this descent it seems to have passed to William T. Williams, the son of William Williams, and brother of the wife of John McClellan, who in turn received it and added his autograph, from whom it passed to its present owner, Mr. Joseph McClellan, of Woodstock.

It is possible, and perhaps probable, that some other of the four hundred books of Brewster's library may yet be found, and I venture to add to these remarks a transcript of their titles from the Plymouth Records, not only as indicative of the kind of library which he had, but as possibly assisting hereafter in the identification of some of them. It is well known that Brewster's press was active at Leyden in printing books that the censors in England condemned. The subject may very likely be further elucidated as to the extent of such printing if many other volumes in this inventory are found; but we may be quite content to leave such investigations in the hands of Dr. Dexter. I have asked his permission to quote a passage in a recent letter which came to me from him: —

"In January, 1876, after much effort I succeeded in purchasing for twenty-five dollars, of the late Charles Hammond, of Monson, a small volume in a dilapidated condition, which he had picked up in some Connecticut garret, the interest of which to me consisted in the fact that, among other things, it included a perfect copy of John Robinson's 'Peoples' Plea.' It was loosely stitched together in a manner to make me think it might be the 'divers books sticht together' of the inventory, and priced two shillings. The first thing I did was to cut it apart, when I had before me seven small 16mo's, five of which were perfect. When laid side by side, I was immediately struck with their similar type, the same sized page, the same ornaments, and with that indescribable *tout ensemble* which declares the same printing-house. They were all of date 1618 and 1619, except that the seventh lacked the title; and this and the others were of the same office, as the worn and somewhat broken type showed. My next step was to infer, as I had always heard that the 'Plea' was printed by Elder Brewster at Leyden, that they all might have been. I then set to work to see what evidence there may be that the 'Plea' was really printed by Brewster. It has two large initial letters, each defective slightly in spots, and by comparing these (with a microscope) with like initials in books known to have been printed by Brewster at Leyden, I arrived at a moral certainty that all were his. Of such books I have three of which I suppose no reasonable doubt can be entertained, namely, 'Commentarii Succincti & Dilucidi in Proverbia Salomonis,' which has his imprint, 'Lvgdvni Batavorvm. Apud Gulielmum Brevvsterum. In vico Chorali, 1617;' Cartwright's 'A Confvtation of the Rhemists Translation, Glosses and Annotations on the Nevv Testament,' (with no imprint), 1618; and the 'Perth Assembly' (no imprint), 1619. Both the latter seem well authenticated by Sir Dudley Carleton's Letters (pp. 379, 380, 390). The 'Proverbia' has but two large initials, but the 'Confutation' has twenty-six, and the 'Assembly' has six, — thirty-two in all, — offering a fair chance for comparison. As the result of a careful study of the matter, I feel morally certain that the whole ten books were printed at the same press between 1617 and 1619 inclusive, and that that press was William Brewster's."

I may be pardoned in adding a final sentence from Dr. Dexter's letter, indicative of his laborious study in the literature of the Pilgrims. He says: —

"I have never till this year succeeded in getting together what might be called a perfect set of John Robinson's original editions; yet even now I lack his 'Manvmission to a Manvdvction' (1615), which Mr. Deane has, and his 'Appeal on Truth's Behalf,' which nobody seems to have but the Bodleian. I have abandoned all hope of ever getting his 'Answer to a Censorious Epistle,' or 'Catechism' except as published with the 1644 edition of his 'Apologie.'"

I may finally add that I found the other day, on running over the titles of John Harvard's books, — part of his endowment of the College, the list of which is preserved in the College Records, — that Harvard had, among these companions of his pilgrimage to New England, the Essays of John Robinson, the Pilgrim Pastor.

The inventory of the library of Elder Brewster in the Plymouth Records is as follows: —

		£	s.	d.
It	2 little chatachismes	00—00—04		
It	1 Lambeth on the Will of man	00—00—02		
It	1 morrall discourse	00—00—02		
It	Discouery of Spanish Inquisition	00—00—03		
It	Johnson on 18th Math	00—00—04		
It	Remaynes of Brittaine	00—01—00		
It	Description of New England	00—00—04		

An Inventory of the Latten books taken by Mr. Bradford Mr Prence and Mr Reyner May 18th 1644.[1]

		£	s.	d.
Inpris	Nova Testamenti Malarato	01—04—00		
It	Tromelius & Junius Biblia Sacra	00—18—00		
It	Beza noua testament, lat & gre	01—00—00		

[1] The title of the Inventory is thus interjected in the Records.

		£	s.	d.
It	Centuria Selecta	00	08	00
It	Calvin duodecim ꝑphet	00	15	00
It	Clauis Scriptura flacio Illirico	00	15	00
It	Peter Martyr Com. prio' ad Corinthos	00	08	00
It	Musculus ad Isaiam & Romanos	00	12	00
It	Regneri prandinī	00	02	06
It	Œcolumnadī in Jeremia	00	03	00
It	Crisostm Mattias & Joannes	00	06	00
It	Musculus Psalmos David	00	12	00
It	Caluī at Daniel	00	05	00
It	Calvī on Isaȳ	00	15	00
It	Musculus ambos Epist ad Corinthos	00	08	00
It	Molleri ad Psalmos	00	10	00
It	Lanaterus Esequeh	00	05	00
It	Zanchī ad Ephe	00	06	00
It	Syntagma amudo polo Syntagmatis theologia Christian	00	10	00
It	Sulteti Isaiam	00	05	00
It	Purei Hoseam	00	01	00
It	Gualterin Deluerin Nov Test	00	02	06
It	Psalm Pagnii	00	02	06
It	Pareus in Genosa	00	08	06

11 . 05 . 00

		£	s.	d.
It	Piscator in Nova Testament	00	17	00
It	Pareus ad Romanos	00	05	00
It	Pareus ad Priorem Corinthis	00	04	00
It	Calvin Eze. vigint prima	00	03	00
It	Tabula Analytice Stephano	00	01	06
It	Cartwright harmã 4 Evanğl	00	05	00
It	Pascillia Hemnigm	00	01	00
It	De Vera Jes. Chr. Religione	00	01	00
It	Erasmus in Marciñ	00	01	06
It	Parkerius politica Eccle	00	05	00
It	Piscator in Genešn	00	02	00
It	Kykermano Systema Physica	00	03	00
It	Beza Confess. Christ	02	02	04
It	Rollock in Dany	00	02	06
It	Dauen in priõ Juni	00	02	00
It	Thom Thomaseus Dix	00	02	00
It	Bastwick Apolegeticus	00	00	06
It	Machauelii princeps	00	01	08
It	Elenchus papistice Bastwick	00	00	06

		£	s.	d.
It	Rollock at Psalmos	00	02	06
It	Rainoldi de Romana Eccles	00	02	06
It	Calvin in Josua	00	01	00
It	Syntagma Vigandus	00	01	06
It	Epistola Apologetica	00	01	06
It	Paraphrasa Erasmus in Luke	00	01	06
It	Latina gramatica	00	00	06
It	Hebrew Gramat	00	00	06
It	Camden Brittan	00	03	00
It	Rollock ad Romanos Ephes	00	03	00
It	Dixtio. Triglott	00	01	06
It	Buxtorff Lexicon	00	04	06
It	Cartwright prouerbia	00	07	00
It	Junii ad Ecclām Dei	00	00	03
It	Tyrocinia	00	00	04
It	Poemata Heringii	00	00	02
It	Ad Reuerend. patres Eclles Anglican	00	00	06
It	Amesii contra Grevin. Co.	00	00	06
It	Hypomneses	00	00	03
It	Antichristus prognostica	00	00	04
It	Harmonia Evangelia	00	00	06

15 . 19 . 04

An inventory of the English books taken by Mr Bradford & Mr. Prence.

		£	s.	d.
It	1 English bible lattin letter	00	08	00
It	1 English bible	00	06	00
It	A new Testament	00	05	00
It	Mr Ainsworths Psalms in prose & meter	00	02	00
It	1 new testament	00	01	04
It	Major Coment new testament	00	12	00
It	Hexapla upon Daniell	00	05	00
It	2 volumes of Mr Perkins	01	10	00
It	Mr Hernes works	00	05	00
It	Babingtons works	00	08	00
It	Cartwright against Remisc	00	08	00
It	Byfield on Coloss	00	05	00
It	Dodoner Herball	00	06	00
It	Mr Rogers on Judges	00	06	00
It	Mr Richardson on yᵉ State of Eur	00	04	00
It	Knights Concord	00	05	00
It	Caluin on Isay	00	06	00
It	Willet on Romans	00	06	00

		£	s.	d.
It	Grensames works	00	10	00
It	Bodens Comon weale	00	08	00
It	Willet on the 1st Samuel	00	04	00
It	Surveyor by Ratborne	00	03	00
It	Willet on Genesis	00	07	00
It	Seneca Workes	00	06	00
It	Wilcocks on Psalmes	00	06	00
It	Cotton's Concordance 2 volumes	00	12	00
It	Scholastical discourse about the crofse	00	04	00
It	Taylor upon Tytus	00	05	00
It	Hill upon life Euer	00	05	00
It	Wilson's Dixonor	00	06	00
It	Waimes Christiã Synagogue	00	02	00
It	Gibbines question & disputacons	00	02	06
It	Calvin Harmon Evan.	00	06	00
It	Defence of Synod of Dort by Robin	00	02	00
It	Mefselina	00	03	01
It	Downams Warfarr 2 ℣t	00	04	00
It	Barlow on 2 Tymothy	00	02	06
It	Cartwights agst Whitgift 2 ℣t	00	02	00
It	Jackson agst Misbeleefe	00	02	00
It	Granger on Eccl.	00	02	00
It	Brightman on Reuel.	00	05	00
It	Birdag Anti	00	02	00
It	Byfield on 1 Peter	00	05	00
It	Weymes on Image of God in Man	00	02	00
It	Parr on Romans	00	05	00
It	Robinsons Observacons	00	02	00
It	Right way to go to worke	00	02	00
It	Byfield's sermons on 1 Peter	00	05	00
It	Dod on Commandmts	00	02	06
It	Mayor on Catholick Epistles	00	03	00
It	Taylor parable on the Sower	00	02	00
It	Narme of Chr. Strarr	00	02	00
It	Morley of truth of religion	00	03	00
It	Attersons badges of Christianity	00	02	00
It	Downam Consolatrix	00	03	00
It	Elton on 7 Romans	00	02	00
It	A declaracon of Quintill. question	00	02	00
It	Byfield on 3 of Peter	00	01	06
It	7 prbleames against Antechrist	00	01	00
It	Dike upon Repent	00	01	06
It	Sibbs Soules Comfort	00	03	06

		£	s.	d.
It	Passions of the mynd	00	01	06
It	5 bookes of Sermons stichet together	00	01	00
It	Constitucons & Cannons of ff of Cant.	00	00	02
It	Wittenhall discovery of abuses	00	01	00
It	Rollock on Thessal	00	02	00
It	Heauen opened by Coop	00	02	00
It	Treasury of smiles	00	04	00
It	Downefall of Popery	00	02	00
It	Saints by calling by Wilson	00	02	00
It	Wittenhall discoũy of abuses	00	02	00
It	Udall on Lamentacons	00	01	04
It	Dyocean Tryall	00	00	06
It	Sparks against Albin	00	02	06
It	Wottons defence of Perkins Refor Catholicke	00	02	06
It	Brinslow on Ezech	00	03	00
It	Defence of Ministers reasons	00	01	06
It	Downam agst Bath & Wells	00	01	06
It	A discourse of troubles Chu. of Amster.	00	01	06
It	Mr Smyths 3 treatises	00	02	06
It	Discourse of equivocation	00	01	06
It	Mr Smyths paroliles	00	00	08
It	A peticon for reformacõn	00	00	06
It	A primer of Chr. Relig.	00	00	09
It	A discourse of variance betweene pope and Venet.	00	01	00
It	Broughton on Lament.	00	01	00
It	Perkins on Sat. Sophist	00	00	06
It	A discourse of adoracõn of Reliq^{us}	00	01	00
It	A trew mark of Catholike Church	00	00	06
It	A quodlibet to bewarr of preise	00	00	04
It	Justifycacon of sepacõn	00	02	00
It	Storke answere to Campion	00	02	00
It	Dike on the heart	00	02	00
It	Perkins on 11 Hebrewes	00	03	02
It	Bayne on Ephes	00	02	00
It	Dike on repent. & ch. temtations	00	02	00
*It	Bolton on true happynes	00	01	06
It	Downam agst Beller	00	01	08
It	Wotton on 1 John	00	02	00
It	Gouge Armor of God	00	02	00
It	Plea for Infants	00	01	06
It	Dod on Commandm^{ts}	00	03	00
It	Rollock on effectual calling	00	01	10
It	Calling of Jews by Finish.	00	01	00

		£	s.	d.
It	Prin Antearminescence	00	00	08
It	Discouery by Barrow	00	03	00
It	Ainsworths defence of Scripture	00	01	06
It	2 Downam's Reply agst Bath	00	03	00
It	Admonition to Parli^{nt}	00	01	06
It	Refutacon to Gifford	00	02	06
It	Perth Assembly	00	01	06
It	Defence of the Ministers reasons	00	01	06
It	Treatise of Ministery of England	00	01	00
It	Cassander Anglicañs	01	01	08
It	Downams warfarr	00	05	00
It	The meane of mourneing	00	03	00
It	Hackhill History of Judges	00	00	00
It	Sweeds Intelligencer	00	01	06
It	Comunion of Saints	00	02	00
It	Abridgment of Ministers of Lincolne	00	01	06
It	Jacob Attestation	00	01	00
It	Modest defence	00	03	00
It	Exposicon of Canticles	00	01	00
It	Whitgifte answere to a libell	00	01	00
It	A reply to a libell	00	02	00
It	Duplefs of a Chur.	00	02	00
It	Perkins on Iude	00	02	00
It	Downams 4 treatises	00	02	00
It	Deareing on Hebrews	00	03	00
It	A Collection of Englands Delĩuanc^{s}	00	01	06
It	1000 notable things	00	01	06
It	Riches of elder ages	00	00	00
It	Dod on comandm^{ts}	00	02	06
It	Sweeds Intilligencer	00	01	06
It	tymes turne coate	00	00	06
It	A continuacon of adventur of Don Sebastian	00	00	04
It	Surveyor Dialougs	00	01	00
It	Apology Chur. of England agst Brownists	00	01	06
It	Kings declaracon about Parli^{nts}	00	00	02
It	Scyrge of Drunkerds	00	00	02
It	Syons Plea	00	02	00
It	Elton of Comandmts.	00	02	00
It	Treatise of Chr. Religion	00	02	00
It	A battaile of Palatinate	00	01	06
It	Treatise 122 Psalm	00	00	06
It	Concordance of yeares	00	00	06
It	Cesars Tryumphs	00	00	02

		£	s.	d.
It	A dialogue concerneing Ceremonies	00	00	04
It	Essayes about a prisoner	00	00	03
It	Politike diseases	00	00	06
It	Exposicon of Liturgie	00	00	08
It	Magnifycent entertaynement of King James	00	00	06
It	A modest defence	00	00	06
It	Essex practise of treason	00	00	06
It	Prosopeia	00	00	02
It	Withers motto	00	00	04
It	Standish for woods	00	00	06
It	A recantacon of a Brownist	00	00	04
It	A supply to German History	00	01	00
It	Of the use of silk worms	00	00	06
It	Newes from Virginia	00	00	06
It	Newes from Palatinate	00	00	04
It	Hacklett	00	02	00
It	Byfeild on the oracles of God	00	03	02
It	Gods monarchy Deuells Kingdome	00	00	04
It	New shreds of old share	00	00	06
It	Discharg of 5 imputacons	00	01	00
It	Dauids Musick	00	00	06
It	Horne sheild of the Rightous	00	01	00
It	Ruine of Rome	00	01	06
It	Downame on 15 Psalm	00	01	06
It	Pisca Evangelica	00	01	06
It	Virell on Lords prayer	00	01	06
It	Answere to Cartwright	00	00	06
It	Broughton on Gods Diuinitie	00	01	00
It	Bayne tryall of Christ state	00	01	06
It	Wheatley on Gods husbandry	00	01	00
It	Exposicon on Reuelac	00	01	00
It	Perkins Reformed Catholik	00	01	06
It	Johnsons & Withers works	00	02	00
It	10 sermons of the supper	00	01	06
It	Ciuill Conuersacon Gnahzo	00	02	00
It	Smyths plea for Infants	00	00	06
It	Bacons p'ficiency in Learning	00	02	00
It	Arguments agst seinge	00	01	06
It	Theologicks	00	00	06
It	Eming on James	00	01	06
It	Catholike Judg	00	01	00
It	The spirituall watch	00	01	00
It	reasons for reformacon of Chur of Engl	00	00	06

		£	s.	d.
It	A looking glass agst Prelates	00	01	00
It	A sermon of Bishop of London	00	00	06
It	Resolucon for kneeling	00	00	06
It	2 Exact discouery of Romish doctrine	00	00	04
It	Warr was a blefsing	00	00	06
It	Midland souldier	00	00	04
It	Humillitie Christians life	00	00	06
It	Church Deliûance	00	01	00
It	Coment on Ecclesiastic	00	00	06
It	Prerogatiue of Parli^{nts}	00	00	06
It	Temple on 20 Psalm	00	01	06
It	Abbott sermon	00	00	03
It	Soules Implantacon	00	03	04
It	A treatise of Stage pleas.	00	00	03
It	Apologue of Brownists	00	00	04
It	State Mistery of Jesuits	00	00	06
It	Dike Schoole of affliccon	00	02	00
It	Sibbs Comfort	00	01	06
It	Taylor on 32 psalm	00	02	00
It	Parable of the Vine by Rogers	00	02	00
It	Apologeticall reply by Damfort	00	02	00
It	divers books sticht to-gether	00	02	00
It	Broughton of Lamentacons	00	00	06
It	A good wyfe	00	00	03
It	Northbrook against Images	00	01	06
It	Tryall of truth by Chibbald	00	01	00
It	The tryall of truth	00	00	04
It	The paterne of true prayer	00	01	06
It	Houshold gouerment	00	01	06
It	Blackwells answers	00	00	04
It	Aristotles probleames	00	00	06
It	Symers Indictment	00	00	04
It	Johnsons psalmes n meeter	00	00	04
It	Mores discouery	00	00	03
It	A sermon	00	00	02
It	Refutacon of tolleracon	00	00	06
It	Aphorismes of state	00	00	02
It	Of Union betweene England & Scotland	00	00	06
It	Tales of Popes custome house	00	00	04
It	Of Pope Joane	00	00	04
It	A dialogue betweene a gent & a preist	00	00	04
It	Against kneeleing	00	00	03
It	Perkins on fayth	00	00	03

		£	s.	d.
It	Bacons Apologye	00	00	03
It	A History of Mary Glouer	00	00	03
It	A bundle of smale books & papers	00	02	00
It	Defyance of death	00	01	00
It	A Christians apparelling	00	01	06
It	Perkins on repentanc	00	00	08
It	Essays by Cornwallis	00	01	06
It	Spirituall stedfastnes	00	00	08
It	A manuell	00	00	06
It	A breiffe of bible	00	00	06
It	Jacob on 2ᵈ Comandⁿᵗ	00	00	04
It	A pill to purge popery	00	00	02
It	Withers	00	00	04
It	Cathologue of nobillyty of England	00	00	03
It	English votaryes	00	00	06
It	Sibbs Yea & Amen	00	01	06
It	Sermons by Rollock	00	01	00
It	Kinges Bath	00	00	08
It	Great Afsise by Smyth	00	00	08
It	Martin on Easter	00	01	00
It	Smyth on 6ᵗʰ of Hosea	00	01	06
It	Discription of World	00	01	00
It	Cantelus Cannon of Mafse	00	01	00
It	Perkins of Repentance	00	00	06
It	Gods m̄cy & Jurasa misery	00	00	06
It	Silũ Watch bell	00	00	06
It	7 sermons by W. B.	00	00	06
It	Burton agˢᵗ Cholmely	00	00	06
It	Sibbs Saints pʳuiledges	00	01	01
It	Sibbs Riches of mercy	00	01	01
It	Regla vitᵉ	00	01	01
It	Pilgrimes pʳfession	00	00	08
It	Sermon at Pauls crofse	00	00	04
It	Nature & grace	00	00	00
It	Perkins of Predestinacon	00	00	06
It	Spirituall trumpett	00	00	08
It	Vox Regis	00	00	06
It	Barrowes platforme	00	00	06
It	Exposicon of Lords prayer	00	00	06
It	Comon weale of England	00	00	06
It	Right way of peace	00	00	06
It	4ᵗʰ pt of true watch	00	01	00
It	Johnson on Psalms	00	01	00

		£	s.	d.
It	Byfeild paterne of	00	01	00
It	Duke promises	00	00	06
It	A help to memorye	00	00	06
It	pposicons by John Sprint	00	00	11
It	The morality of law	00	00	06
It	Cases of Conscience by Per	00	01	00
It	Discouery of famyly of love	00	00	06
It	Sermon of repentance	00	00	06
It	Sermon at Pauls crosse	00	00	06
It	Sibbs spirituall maxims	00	00	09
It	Memorable conceits	00	01	00
It	God & the Kinge	00	00	04
It	Smyth on Riddle of Nebuchudnez.	00	00	08
It	Estey on Comandnts & 51st Psalm	00	01	00
It	Christians dayly walk	00	01	06
It	Exposicon of 11 & 12 Revelacon	00	00	06
It	Treatise of English medicines	00	00	06
It	A dialogue of desiderias	00	00	06
It	A supplycacon to the King	00	00	06
It	Abba father	00	00	06
It	Abrahams tryall discourse	00	01	00
It	Jacobbs ladder	00	01	06
It	Perkins of Imagina	00	00	06
It	Burton Christl question	00	00	06
It	A toyle for 2 legged foxes	00	00	06
It	A cordiall for comfort	00	00	06
It	Zacheus conuersion	00	02	01
It	Spirituall touchstone	00	00	03
It	Dearmies advantage	00	00	06
It	Englands summons	00	00	06
It	Burton wooing his Church	00	00	04
It	Goulden Key	00	01	00
It	A remedy against famine & warr	00	00	06
It	Treatise against popery	00	01	00
It	Treatise of Gods religion	00	00	08

The totall of both Latten & English books amounts to
the sum of .... 42—19—11
The totall of both goods & bookes amounts in all to 150—00—07

WM. BRADFORD.
THO. PRENCE.

Printed in the USA
CPSIA information can be obtained
at www.ICGtesting.com
CBHW072312250824
13685CB00025BA/71